PEOPLE OF THE BREAKING DAY

written and illustrated by Marcia Sewall

Aladdin Paperbacks
New York London Toronto Sydney New Delhi

ACKNOWLEDGMENTS

I wish to thank Daisy Moore—Whispering Waters—of Mingo/Mye, Inc., for her helpful suggestions; Barbara Norton and Theresa Furfey, who gave me invaluable material at the beginning of this journey; friends at the Codman Square Branch of the Boston Public Library for their gracious assistance; Pat Cleaveland for her time and encouragement; The Workshop group; my editor, Marcia Marshall, for her good judgment; my mother, for sharing her love of nature with me; and Peter, my Sunday landscape painting friend, for our many excursions to look at sunlight and shadow.

The quote on page 3 is found in Indian New England Before the Mayflower, *by Howard S. Russell, published by University Press of New England.*

First Aladdin Paperbacks edition September 1997
Copyright © 1990 by Marcia Sewall

Aladdin Paperbacks
An imprint of Simon & Schuster Children's Publishing Division
1230 Avenue of the Americas, New York, NY 10020

Also available in an Atheneum Books for Young Readers edition.
Manufactured in China

8   10   9   7

The Library of Congress has cataloged the hardcover edition as follows:
Sewall, Marcia.
People of the breaking day / by Marcia Sewall. — 1st ed.
p.   cm.
Summary: A poetic evocation of the life-style and traditional beliefs of the Wampanoag Indians.
ISBN 0-689-31407-8
1. Wampanoag Indians—Juvenile literature.   [1. Wampanoag Indians.   2. Indians of North America.]   I. Title.
E99.W2S49   1990
305.8'973—dc20
89-18194
CIP   AC

ISBN 978-0-689-31407-0 (hc.)
ISBN 978-0-689-81684-0 (Aladdin pbk.)
0422 SCP

In memory of Steve Howe

"With all beings and all things we shall be as brothers."

OUR TRIBE

We are Wampanoags, People of the Breaking Day. Nippa'uus, the Sun, on his journey through the sky, warms us first as he rises over the rim of the sea. At his birth each new morning we say, "Thank you, Nippa'uus, for returning to us with your warmth and light and beauty."

But it is Kiehtan, the Great Spirit, who made us all: we, the two-legged who stand tall, and the four-legged; those that swim and those that fly and the little people who crawl; and flowers and trees and rocks. He made us all, brothers sharing the earth. From the birds and beasts and fish, we, the two-legged, will each choose a guardian spirit, our manitou for life.

We who stand tall admire the keen sight of the hawk. We have learned to sweep the woods with our eyes and catch movement there. We appreciate the stealth of the fox as he stalks his prey, and we, too, have learned to tread silently. We know the tracks left by animal footprints and have learned how to hide our own. We respect the four-leggeds' keen sense of smell, for they always know our whereabouts unless we smoke our bodies by burning sage or sweet grass. And, like fish, we swim.

We are a nation of people, a large family of several thousand people. We speak the same language. We worship the same spirits. We live in small settlements never too far from the sea, where the sun rises.

Our many villages are within a day's run of each other. Paths, like sinew, bind them together. The people of our villages may hunt and fish together in season. For planting, we may gather to help each other break up fields. And how much we look forward to spring—warm days again

and plentiful food again! Then we will come together to celebrate a season of plenty.

When corn silks darken in the Neepunnakee'wush moon, once more we shall gather to celebrate this gift of food. We will build a dance house many, many feet long and, for a week, dance and sing and play games together and eat plenty, but first we will place a pot of precious corn on the hot coals to burn and, in smoke, to mingle with the spirit powers.

It was Crow who came to us long ago from the direction of the warm wind, home of Kiehtan, the Great Spirit, carrying a corn seed and a bean seed in his ears. We thank him for his gifts. No longer must we roam about the earth always searching for food. Now we plant a garden.

Every year when the Sequanakee'wush moon comes around again, and warm rains fall upon the earth again, and the Thunder Beings shake the sky, it is planting time. If warm rains stop falling and our seeds

do not grow, we will climb the sacred hill and pray to the Great Spirit and ask him to favor us with rain. And if the sun does not shine, we will climb the sacred hill and ask the Great Spirit to favor us with sun. If he is pleased with us, rain will follow sun and sun will follow rain. Our seeds will grow and we shall have food. Then we will survive when cold winds howl and snow blankets the earth, when bears sleep and we grow lean.

Our great sachem is Massasoit, a man of peace, who became our leader upon his father's death. And so it will be. For Wamsutta, Massasoit's oldest son, one day shall lead our people. Our great sachem knows the fields and forests and waters where our tribe can hunt and fish and grow crops. He decides upon our just punishment if the rules of our people are broken. And it is our great sachem and his council of warriors who decide when we should make war. Lesser sachems advise our great leader of the needs of each small settlement within the large Wampanoag nation.

Narragansetts and Nausets, Nipmucks and Massachusetts, Pequots and Niantics are other tribes that live near us, with their own sachems and their own lands for hunting and fishing. Farther away live Penacooks and Abanakis, Mohawks and Mahicans. We are sometimes at war with each other and sometimes at peace. Our braves may fight for a good hunting ground or fishing stream or berry patch, and they are quick to avenge a wrong deed. When our sons are sixteen winters old and have proved their bravery, they can become warriors.

In preparation for war, we who are warriors paint ourselves fiercely. We mix colors with animal grease to make paint: black from charcoal; red, in springtime, from the juice of bloodroot plants and, in fall, from black currant berries; white from clay found in the riverbed; and green from young shoots of elder bushes.

The night before a battle, we dance a dance of war and beat the ground with sticks and pierce the sky with war cries. Our pulses quicken. At dawn we drink a strong juniper-berry tea to help our blood clot if we should be wounded. Then we ask the spirit powers to make us

swift as the deer, cunning as the fox, and may our poisoned arrows find their marks. We are ready to fight.

Since boyhood we have been trained to be proud and courageous; to run many miles a day; to endure pain and cold and tainted foods; to be calm and silent and strong. If wounded, like our animal brothers we will lie with our wound against Mother Earth and she will try to heal us. If captured, we are prepared to suffer and die. We are proud of our bravery. For a great coup a warrior will place another eagle feather in his shiny black hair.

When at peace we eagerly trade with other people. We especially prize the Narragansetts' soapstone pipes and bowls and wampum; delicate purple and white beads made from quahog shells found in their waters. We trade these pipes and bowls and beads, and our own wooden bowls and corn seed with the Abanakis north of us for their birch bark, which we will make into lightweight canoes. And we will trade what we have with people many sleeps away for their pretty fire-lit copper and their sharp-cutting flints.

In peacetime, we play fair games with the other nations. Our men love to gather in a crowd and gamble. *"Hub! Hub! Hub!"* they cry, hoping for a winning throw of their black-and-white bone dice. On vast distances of sand by the sea, our men, disguised in war paint, play a rough game of ball. It may take days, and even a few broken bones, before the ball is kicked over a goalpost and the game won! We love a good footrace and we enjoy matching our skill with bows and arrows. When our games are over, we say *"Hawu'nshech"* and part as peaceful neighbors.

A FAMILY

Our father, brave and strong and wise, is always our gentle teacher. He observes Nippa'uus, the Sun, and Munna'mock, the Moon, and the stars. He feels the Wind Spirits as they change places. He, at all times, watches the shape of clouds and the colors of the sea. As a brother of all plants and animals, he knows them well and with great knowledge makes decisions that will affect our lives. When and where we move is most important to the survival of our family. If we go to high land, we will see all that is about us. If our village is surrounded by swamp, then we are well hidden from our enemies. But wherever we go, there must be firewood nearby. He talks about these matters with the leader of our village, who then holds council with the leader of our tribe.

Much time our father spends making arrows from hardwood saplings with points carefully shaped of bone or flint or eagle claw; and bows, tall as a man, from strong, flexible wood strung with sinew. Many days he will prepare for the hunt. For a deer drive, miles of fence must be cut and put in place so that the deer will run to a small opening and into his swift arrows. For trapping, snares must be laid. For fishing, he must shape hooks and spears from bone and wood. From hemp, twisted and braided, he makes fish line. He will weave purse nets for scooping up fish, and long gill nets in which to entangle them. He will make a

mishoo'n shaped from a tall chestnut or pine tree. Slowly he will burn and scrape and hollow the wood, making a gouge fit for men to sit in. Then he will paddle out onto the open sea or down the beautiful rivers, there to catch fish.

He will cut long sapling poles, pound them into the earth, then bend and tie them together to make the frame of our *wetu*. And the men of our village will build a smokehouse and a sweat lodge. Men leave the labor of gardening to women, except for their prized plots of *ottomma'ocke*.

Our mother cares for our needs and is patient with us as we grow. It is she who tends our planting fields. It is she who prepares and preserves our food. Her capable hands turn deerskin into clothes and weave our mats and baskets. Her strong back carries our shelter and belongings from place to place, and we, her daughters, help her. We love to listen to her songs, full of thanks for life and for earth's gifts.

We, the children of our family, roam over the fields and along the shore. We play in the brook and we are constantly in and out of the pond. We especially like to skirt the edges of the forest and make small wigwams there. We are eager to know about everything that we see and hear and smell.

In the Namassackee'wush moon, when river ice has gone, when ducks and geese return to Father Sky and bring back the east wind that melts the snow, it is time for our family to return to the fishing place. Fish, again, will swim from the deep sea up the swift-moving rivers and over the falls to lay their eggs. Our men now catch them in their purse nets. It is a time of plenty.

Now our mother will move our belongings from the wintering place to the fishing stream and, soon, on to the planting fields as the days lengthen. On her back in a cradleboard rides a little *papoo's*, coated with a layer of animal grease for warmth and wrapped in soft skins. Only our family and the leaders of our tribe will know her true name, for names are sacred. People will call her by her nickname, Little Sweet Red Berry.

When we arrive at the planting fields, our first job, as children, is

to fetch water from the spring nearby. Then, after we collect firewood, one of the boys will make a dancing flame with his fire bow and light the dry kindling. There will be fish in the stream not far away and plenty of squirrels in the trees and perhaps a foraging turkey to be hunted. At the shore nearby there are clams to be dug. Now our mother will put together a meal, for we are hungry! Into the pot of cooking food she will throw a little cornmeal for nourishment and thickening, and some clam broth for flavoring.

Setting up our *wetu* this spring will not be difficult, for the bent sapling poles, used last year, still remain standing beside the planting fields. Our mother will lash cattail-stem wall coverings to those poles with cord she has made from pounded and twisted bark, leaving a low opening for a door. Next, she will cover the inside walls with mats carefully woven of bulrushes, and on the tamped-down earth place mats for us to sleep upon. In time, our father may make some low bed racks. Though at the top of our *wetu* is a smoke hole, there are days when our dwelling is smoky and our eyes burn. Often we prefer to sleep with our animal brothers under the night sky.

When white oak leaves bud, it is time for our mother again to set corn. If there is little new spring growth in the old cornfield, we know the earth is tired. Then our father will clear more land with his stone ax and sacred fire and make another sunny garden place for growing seeds.

Last year, as always, our mother saved out the best formed ears of *ewa'chim* for seed, pulled back the husks, and braided them together, allowing them to dry. During three moons she will plant those seeds. For three moons she will harvest them. In each small mound of earth, hoed with a quahog-shell hoe, she will first place herring or chopped-up horseshoe crabs to rot and nourish the soil. Within a double handful of sleeps, with her planting stick barely disturbing Mother Earth, she will poke holes in the soil and plant, in each mound, four corn and two bean seeds. Nearby she will plant a patch of pumpkins.

We, the children of our family, will spend our days now at the

planting fields, for we must shoo away birds who come to feast on the newly planted seeds. But we are always careful not to harm our friend Crow.

Our garden is easy to tend. As cornstalks grow tall, sprouting beans will climb the stalks and reach for sun. In between the hills of corn, our mother plants squash and cucumber seeds. They will spread their broad leaves across the warm earth, holding moisture in the soil and keeping weeds down. We listen at night to the dogs barking. They are hunting raccoons in our cornfield. We are grateful for their watchful spirit.

Now it is time to help our mother dig clay from the riverbed. The sun is hot on our backs and we happily swim to wash off. Then we must drag the heavy clay home. We watch the women of our village knead the clay and shape it into beautiful pots, then take a scrap of shell and carefully draw a pattern into the hardening surface. We can't resist taking a bit of clay to make a few dogs and dolls and a dugout canoe. After we dry what we have made, we put those things on hot coals to harden them.

Our mother often goes to the shore to dig clams and we, who are

her daughters, help her. In preparation for winter, we will cook the shucked *sicki'ssuog* on sweet green sticks over an open fire. We will also spear and roast large crabs and lobsters, and dry fish on racks in the sun or smoke them in smokehouses, along with eels and animal flesh. The smell of the delicious smoked foods fills our heads. We taste a bit of everything and store the rest. In red cedar baskets and animal-skin bags, deep in earth pits dug by our men, we will bury our preserved food. Let the cold winds bite! Let snow fall deep around our winter dwelling! We know what Mother Earth holds for us.

During the growing season we who are women, young and old, gather plants for medicine and for food. We know just where we can find groundnuts and wild rice and sea lettuce, which we will add to a nourishing stew. In the woods we know where to find shiny wintergreen leaves, which we will grind fine and mix with animal grease to be rubbed into the aching joints of our old people. In baskets we gather many sorts of bark. Our bonesetter will make splints of heavy bark, and birch bark and pine bark are soothing to burns.

We who are children love to dive for water-lily roots to be dried and pounded into a healing powder. Nearby we pull up skunk cabbage. Formed into a poultice, it is good for toothaches! In the forest we collect acorns from the white oak tree, and chestnuts, and in sunny places we look for berries. Strawberries grow as large as our small hands.

As harvesttime nears, we spend days gathering cattails and hemp and grasses and flexible woods, which we will boil and dry, then weave into mats and wall coverings and baskets of all shapes and sizes.

When the locusts begin to sing, we know that we will have no more than a few handfuls of sleeps before the first frost comes. We must then be sure to gather in our corn and pumpkins, squashes and cucumbers and beans. We thank you, Spirit of the Locust, for your gentle warning.

Throughout the next moons, we, the women of our family, will roast corn and dry corn and grind it into samp, which we will boil with berries. We will make it into bread and pound it into journey-cake meal and parch it and pound it into nourishing nocake meal, which our men always carry tucked into their belt pouches. And, we love the corn that pops! We will mix corn with beans and make succotash. We will throw whole ears of corn, with fish and *sicki'ssuog*, onto stones made hot by fire and bake them under seaweed. We are grateful to you, Crow, for your gift of corn seed.

When the wind beats cold upon our bodies, and again *ho'nckock* and *quequecumau'og* fly away, we, the men of our family, will hunt deer. Like ourselves, deer are fattest at harvesttime. Not only do we need their meat to smoke and dry for winter food, but we must have their skins for clothing, their bladders for bags, their bones for sewing needles and fishhooks, and their tendons for our sinew threads. We are careful to waste nothing that the deer gives to us. We kill only what we need.

Now, when Munna'mock, the Moon, rises round and full, we know it is time for us to catch eels, for they are beginning to swim from the

pond out to sea under the cover of darkness. We will narrow the river with bushes and place our eel traps there to catch them as they pass through the small opening. Thank you, Great Spirit, for making it so.

We have watched the beaver build his dam and his lodge and we know where to find him if we are hungry. Then we will trap him and eat his meat and roast his fat tail and use his fur for warmth. But we are always careful to return his bones to his familiar stream, where, we know, as a beaver, he will live again.

At Pepe'warr, the time of white frost, when leaves sink to the earth in their bright colors, our family returns inland. Away from strong, cold sea winds, our winter longhouse nestles into the protection of a sunny hillside with the forest nearby. Now, the women of the families who share the longhouse will place flattened slabs of dried bark on top of the

woven mats covering the dwelling—another layer to shelter us from the oncoming cold.

As fresh water freezes into thick ice on lakes and ponds, men will chop round holes in the ice and through them spear fish.

It is now that we who are soon to become men are taken blindfolded into the deep forest to be left alone there for the winter with our bow and arrows, a knife and a hatchet, and that is all. As boys we have learned much about survival from our fathers. Still, we will nearly freeze and starve if the winter moons are harsh ones. We will have dreams which, in time, the medicine man will help us understand. We will grow strong and unyielding to cold and pain and hunger. We will learn to know animals as brothers. If we are humbled and made wise, we will grow into leaders of our tribe. Some of us will now become warriors.

Inside the longhouse each of our families is warmed by a fire. When snow and rain keep men from scouring the forest for food, they will spend hours carefully chipping stone against stone to make arrowheads and hatchets. *Muckachuck* will shape arrowheads and hatchets, too. Women will weave dried grasses, stored since summer, into mats and baskets and will pound and twist bark into string and turn animal skins into warm clothing. *Nunsqua*, too, will weave and make string and learn to sew.

If there is food, we will have a pot cooking over the open fire. These are often pleasant hours, filled with good talk and laughter. We are happy living close together, sharing food, sleeping on simple rack beds near the fire. We lie close to one another, with bearskin blankets thrown over our greased and glistening bodies. We love to listen to the old stories of our tribe told by our elders during the long, dark hours. In sleep, we hope for dreams that will give us wisdom. Outside, the Wind Spirits howl and snow blows about us. *Tauh coi!*

We live as our grandfathers' grandfathers have lived forever, rising each day with the rebirth of Nippa'uus, to eat when hungry, to sleep when tired, to gather for celebration, to glean food and do our planting. We, the two-legged, are all equal except for our leader and the shaman, our medicine man. Magic flows through the medicine man like a river connecting what we see to what we cannot see. We cannot see what makes the rain fall. We cannot see what makes a person die. Spirits are everywhere, in everything, and we try not to anger them. If we do, it is the medicine man with his mysterious chants and his medicine bag who comes to help us. Gratefully we pay him with gifts of corn and animal skins and precious beads for his efforts to heal us and keep evil spirits away from our homes.

When we die, we will be wrapped in furs or mats and buried in the evening facing the setting sun with our *mocu'ssinass* in our hands. At our feet will be placed a pot of water; at our head, a basket of meat. These we will need for our journey to the land of Kiehtan, the land where Crow

came from. Those who survive us will blacken their faces and mourn and leave our house empty forever, never to mention our name again. So it has been. So it will always be.

Aque'ne

GLOSSARY

AVENGE—to strike back

BARK—outer layer of a tree

BLADDER—a sac within an animal, which holds body fluids; used by man as containers and balls

BULRUSH—a variety of tall grassy plants that grow in wet places

CATTAIL—a marsh plant having long, straplike leaves and a tall stem

CEDAR—an evergreen tree with an odor unpleasant to insects

CLAM—a type of shellfish

COPPER—a reddish brown metal that is easy to shape into ornaments

CORN SILKS—the tassles found on the tops of ears of corn

COUP—victory

DAY'S RUN—a strong messenger's one-day run, about one hundred miles

FIRE BOW—a friction device used for starting a fire

FLINT—stone that can be easily chipped to a knifelike edge

GLEAN—scrape together

GREEN STICK—a young stick still full of the moisture that prevents it from burning

GROUNDNUT—an edible root that looks like a potato

HEMP—a tall plant with a coarse fiber that can be twisted into string and braided into rope

HERRING—a saltwater fish, small in size

HORSESHOE CRAB—shellfish having a large shelled body and stiff pointed tail

HUSK—the outer covering of an ear of corn

KINDLING—dry sticks of wood that will burn easily

KNEAD—to press and shape with your hands into an even mass

LASH—to tie securely in place

LITTLE PEOPLE—insects

LONGHOUSE—a winter dwelling used by Native Americans in the Northeast, which would shelter from four to eight families, depending on its size

MEDICINE BAG—pouch carried by the medicine man. It held plants, sticks, whistles, and perhaps some part of an animal, which he would magically call upon to cure the sick.

MEDICINE MAN—a person gifted with spiritual powers

MOONS—a means of telling time by months

MOURN—to feel sadness at the death of a loved one

PARCH—to roast over hot ashes

POULTICE—moist mass applied to inflamed part of the body

QUAHOG—large clam

SAGE—strong-smelling plant

SAMP—corn porridge

SAPLING—young tree

SHAMAN—medicine man, a spiritual leader of the tribe

SHUCKED CLAM—clam removed from its shell

SINEW—animal tendons, chewed till soft, then twisted into thread or bowstrings and lashings

SMOKEHOUSE—a temporary structure with open ends, containing racks to hold fish and flesh to be preserved by smoking over an open fire

SNARE—a loop of strong twine assembled to catch animals attracted to some deliberately set food

SOAPSTONE—a stone that can be carved

SWEAT LODGE—a hut with a stone floor on which a fire is built. When the stones are hot, ashes are swept outside and water is poured over the hot stones, creating steam. After an hour of sweating, people leave the sweat lodge and jump into a cold stream or lake nearby. Good for the health.

SWEET GRASS—a sweet-smelling grass

TAINTED—poisoned

TAMPED-DOWN—earth pounded firm

TENDON—a tough tissue that connects bones and muscles

WAMPUM—shell beads used as jewelry and money

WIGWAM—cone- or domed-shaped shelter used by Native Americans of the Northeast

WAMPANOAG/NARRAGANSETT
NATIVE AMERICAN WORDS

aque'ne—peace

ewa'chim—corn

"Hawu'nshech"—"Good-bye"

ho'nckock—geese

"Hub! Hub! Hub!"—"Come! Come! Come!"

mishoo'n—dugout canoe

mocu'ssinass—moccasins, deerskin shoes

muckachuck—boys

Namassackee'wush—March, April; the time of catching fish

Neepunnakee'wush—August, September; when corn is edible

nunsqua—girls

ottomma'ocke—tobacco

papoo's—papoose

Pepe'warr—October, November; white frost

quequecumau'og—ducks

Sequanakee'wush—late April, early May; time to set corn

sicki'ssuog—clams

"Tauh coi!"—"It is very cold!"

wetu—house